THIS BOOK BELONGS TO

_____

START DATE

_____

SHE READS TRUTH

EXECUTIVE

FOUNDER/CHIEF EXECUTIVE OFFICER
Raechel Myers

CO-FOUNDER/CHIEF CONTENT OFFICER
Amanda Bible Williams

CHIEF OPERATING OFFICER
Ryan Myers

EXECUTIVE ASSISTANT
Sarah Andereck

EDITORIAL

CONTENT DIRECTOR
John Greco, MDiv

MANAGING EDITOR
Jessica Lamb

CONTENT EDITOR
Kara Gause

ASSOCIATE EDITORS
Bailey Gillespie
Ellen Taylor

CREATIVE

CREATIVE DIRECTOR
Jeremy Mitchell

LEAD DESIGNER
Kelsea Allen

DESIGNERS
Abbey Benson
Davis DeLisi
Annie Glover

DESIGN INTERN
Brooke Berry

MARKETING

MARKETING DIRECTOR
Hannah Warren

MARKETING MANAGER
Katie Pierce

SOCIAL MEDIA MANAGER
Ansley Rushing

PARTNERSHIP SPECIALIST
Kamiren Passavanti

COMMUNITY SUPPORT SPECIALIST
Margot Williams

SHIPPING & LOGISTICS

LOGISTICS MANAGER
Lauren Gloyne

SHIPPING MANAGER
Sydney Bess

CUSTOMER SUPPORT SPECIALIST
Katy McKnight

FULFILLMENT SPECIALISTS
Abigail Achord
Cait Baggerman
Julia Rogers

SUBSCRIPTION INQUIRIES
orders@shereadstruth.com

CONTRIBUTORS

PHOTOGRAPHERS
Abigail Lewis (38, 49, 52, 66, 79)
Coy Sellers (22)

SPECIAL THANKS
Melanie Rainer

@SHEREADSTRUTH

Download the
She Reads Truth app,
available for iOS
and Android.

Subscribe to the
She Reads Truth podcast

SHEREADSTRUTH.COM

This book was printed offset in Nashville, Tennessee, on 60# Lynx Opaque. Cover is Neenah Avalanche White Stipple 100C.

PSALM 119

WE DELIGHT IN YOUR WORD

IN GOD'S BOOK, I FIND THE STORY OF
HIS LOVE FOR US—A STORY HE HAS
WRITTEN FROM BEGINNING TO END,
FOR OUR GOOD AND HIS GLORY.

Amanda

Amanda Bible Williams
CO-FOUNDER & CHIEF
CONTENT OFFICER

I hope I never forget June 1, 2013. It was a Saturday. I was sitting cross-legged on my bed in our upstairs bedroom while my husband, David, and our three young kids were downstairs doing typical Saturday things. But it was no typical Saturday for me. This was the day God sealed the calling on my heart for this community called She Reads Truth.

"Women in the Word of God every day." That was our mission, both as a collective body of believers and as individual women living our everyday lives in our own corners of the world. We wanted more Jesus, we said. And more Jesus was what we got—not by finally finding a magic formula for our "quiet time" or mastering our spiritual to-do lists, but by opening our Bibles together, right where we were, every day. We'd been doing this for exactly one year. And as I sat in my bedroom that day, watching video after video of women giving testimony to the way God was meeting them in Scripture, I laughed and wept and thanked God for this unparalleled gift.

Over the past eight years, my affection for God's Word has grown from a spark to a steady, unquenchable flame. In God's book, I find comfort for my darkest valley. I find peace in a world that feels upside down and uncertain. I find joy that no circumstance can shake and salvation that cannot be snatched away. I find the gentle, loving rebuke of my Father and the powerful, holy hand of my King. I find a Savior who refuses to let me sit in my sin, turning over tables and dying on a tree to rescue my wayward soul. In God's book, I find the story of His love for us—a story He has written from beginning to end, for our good and His glory.

It is good to delight in God's Word—every part of it. Psalm 119 reminds us of this. A twenty-two stanza love poem to God's law and statutes, Psalm 119 calls us to rejoice in the gift of Scripture and tether our hearts to its instruction. It gives voice to the pendulum swings of the human experience and helps us refocus our trust and affection on the God who does not change.

But delighting in God's Word is not just a posture; it is a practice. That's why our team was excited to add a unique "Delight in the Word" section to the daily readings in this book—an opportunity to practice reading and delighting in different passages of Scripture. You'll also find helpful extras on the gift of Scripture itself, like the timeline of the history of the Bible on page 67 and a look at principles of Bible reading on page 16.

Here at She Reads Truth, "Women in the Word of God every day" is still our singular mission, and this Study Book embodies that mission perhaps more than any other. As you explore Psalm 119, I pray that the beauty, goodness, and truth of God's Word capture your affection in a new way. May each page of Scripture become a lens through which we see clearly God's character and love.

Read on, friends.

DESIGN ON PURPOSE

At She Reads Truth, we believe in pairing the inherently beautiful Word of God with the aesthetic beauty it deserves. Each of our resources is thoughtfully and artfully designed to highlight the beauty, goodness, and truth of Scripture in a way that reflects the themes of each curated reading plan.

For this reading plan, our creative team used the solid, clean font Assistant. We added geometric shapes on top of this existing font to create the stylized Hebrew letters that you'll see at the beginning of each stanza of Psalm 119. These letters represent how the individual, unique words and commands of Scripture come together to provide believers with a full picture of the character of God.

She Reads Truth is a community of women dedicated to reading the Word of God every day.

The Bible is living and active, breathed out by God, and we confidently hold it higher than anything we can do or say. This book focuses primarily on Scripture, with bonus resources to facilitate deeper engagement with God's Word.

SCRIPTURE READING

Designed for a Monday start, this Study Book presents Psalm 119 in daily readings, with supplemental passages for additional context.

DELIGHT IN THE WORD

Each weekday features an additional Scripture passage along with space for reflection. We've chosen a range of passages so you can practice delighting in different parts of Scripture.

GRACE DAY

Use Saturdays to catch up on your reading, pray, and rest in the presence of the Lord.

WEEKLY TRUTH

Sundays are set aside for Scripture memorization.

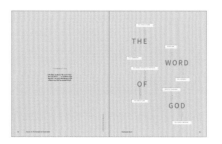

EXTRAS

This book features additional tools to help you gain a deeper understanding of the text.

To see how other Shes and Hes delight in Scripture every day, read the daily devotionals in the **Psalm 119** reading plan at SheReadsTruth.com or on the She Reads Truth app, where women from Columbia to Canada will be reading along with you.

TABLE OF CONTENTS

EXTRAS

WEEK 1

WEEK 2

PSALM 119:114

You are my shelter and my shield;
I put my hope in your word.

PSALM 119

ON THE TIMELINE

The 119th psalm is anonymous and therefore difficult to date with any precision. However, the content of the song indicates an Israelite familiar with the Old Testament Law as its author. The psalm's theme—the blessing and power of God's instruction—is timeless and would fit many different eras of Israelite history.

MESSAGE AND PURPOSE

This psalm is a celebration of God's instruction and, by extension, of God Himself. When reading or singing Psalm 119, one can't help but sense the author's unbridled delight in God's Word as he exults in God's justice and wisdom, His goodness and salvation. At the same time, this song is anything but scattered. It is meticulously organized and restrained. The author carefully chose his form and complied with its structure.

GIVE THANKS FOR PSALM 119

This beautiful psalm gives voice to what so many Bible readers down through the centuries have felt while sitting in the light of God's Word: sheer joy. As a song intended to be sung, Psalm 119 is an invitation to delight in God's ways. And while the psalmist had the commandments of the Old Testament in view, this psalm takes on added significance when we remember that Jesus came to fulfill the Law and that Moses and the prophets spoke of Christ (Mt 5:17).

GOD'S INSTRUCTION

Eight Hebrew terms are used interchangeably throughout Psalm 119 to describe God's instruction. While the Torah (the first five books of the Old Testament) is in focus, what the psalmist writes also applies to everything God has commanded.

TORAH
instruction, *see v. 1*

PIQQUDIM
precept, *see v. 4*

CHOQ
statute, *see v. 5*

MITZVAH
command, *see v. 6*

MISHPAT
judgment, *see v. 7*

DABAR
word, *see v. 9*

IMRAH
word, *see v. 11;* or promise, *see v. 41*

EDUTH
decree, *see v. 22*

THE HEBREW ALPHABET & PSALM 119

Psalm 119 is the longest chapter in the Bible and was written using an acrostic pattern. Each of the twenty-two stanzas corresponds to one letter in the Hebrew alphabet, and every line in each stanza begins with that stanza's letter.

For example, each line of the first stanza (read right to left) begins with the first letter of the Hebrew alphabet, *aleph*. We've shown the first four verses here, alongside two different English translations: the Knox translation, which mimics the Hebrew acrostic pattern by starting each line with the first letter of the English alphabet, "a," and the CSB, a modern translation designed to be both readable and accurate.

א שרי תמימי־דרך ההלכים בתורת יהוה:

Ah, blessed they, who pass through life's journey unstained, who follow the law of the Lord! (Knox Bible)

How happy are those whose way is blameless, who walk according to the L's instruction! (CSB)

א שרי נצרי עדתיו בכל־לב ידרשוהו:

Ah, blessed they, who cherish his decrees, make him the whole quest of their hearts! (Knox Bible)

Happy are those who keep his decrees and seek him with all their heart. (CSB)

אף לא־פעלו עולה בדרכיו הלכו:

Afar from wrong-doing, thy sure paths they tread. (Knox Bible)

They do nothing wrong; they walk in his ways. (CSB)

אתה צויתה פקדיך לשמר מאד:

Above all else it binds us, the charge thou hast given us to keep. (Knox Bible)

You have commanded that your precepts be diligently kept. (CSB)

א ALEPH

ב BETH

ג GIMEL

ד DALETH

ה HE

ו WAW

ז ZAYIN

ח CHETH

ט TETH

י YOD

כ KAPH

ל LAMED

מ MEM

נ NUN

ס SAMEK

ע AYIN

פ PE

צ TSADE

ק QOPH

ר RESH

ש SIN/SHIN

ת TAW

GOD'S WORD IS FOR YOU

The Bible is a gift of immeasurable value. In fact, when the apostle Paul listed the advantages of being born a Hebrew, he put having access to Scripture—"the very words of God"—at the top of the list (Rm 3:2). In Christ, these words of God are ours. The Bible is part of our inheritance. It's our family book; but more importantly, it is an invitation to walk daily with the Lord as we meet with Him in its pages.

The Bible is a diverse library—a collection of documents in many genres and styles, penned by human authors but breathed out by God (2Tm 3:16). We are called to be people of the book, but because of the breadth and scope of Scripture, it can be difficult for followers of Christ to know how to engage with it.

APPROACH GOD'S WORD

APPROACH IT REVERENTLY.

The Bible contains the very words of God, written by men who were "carried along by the Holy Spirit" (2Pt 1:21). It is living and active (Heb 4:12), and we can be confident that when God speaks, His will is accomplished (Is 55:11). This reality should instill in us a sense of respect and awe for the Bible (Ps 111:10).

APPROACH IT CONFIDENTLY.

We are invited to read, study, and meditate on the inspired, complete, and sufficient Word of God with the Author Himself (Jms 4:8). The Bible is for us, given as nourishing food (1Co 3:2; Heb 5:12).

APPROACH IT REGULARLY.

No matter how long we live, we will never be done reading or studying the Bible. It is God's Word to us for every day and in every circumstance. As our relationship with God grows deeper with time, so too should our desire for His Word (Jb 23:12).

ENGAGE GOD'S WORD

ENGAGE IT EXPECTANTLY.

All Scripture is meant to equip us for life with God (2Tm 3:16–17). Therefore, we can read our Bibles with an assurance that God has something for us. We should also expect to find Jesus on every page. Sometimes His presence is obvious (like in the Gospels), and other times it can be more difficult to see (like in Leviticus). But He's there—the promised Rescuer, the healing Teacher, the suffering Messiah, and the returning King (Lk 24:27).

UNDERSTAND GOD'S WORD

UNDERSTAND IT IN CONTEXT.

Before determining what a passage means for us today, we should first understand what it meant for its original audience (2Tm 2:15). The books of the Bible were written in unique cultural contexts, and a basic understanding of these contexts can help guide our thinking.

ENGAGE IT WITH YOUR WHOLE SELF.

In Scripture, we are called to love God with our entire being—heart, soul, strength, and mind (Dt 6:5; Lk 10:27). Similarly, God wants us to engage His Word with everything we are. Time spent in the Bible ought to change us inside and out, transforming our minds and hearts as well as our actions (Rm 12:2; Gl 5:16).

ENGAGE IT BROADLY.

Though it comprises sixty-six books and is further divided into chapters and verses, the Bible is a unified work. We gain new insights reading it from cover to cover, but we also expand our understanding reading entire books in one sitting. It's important to explore how various texts may be related to one another. God is the Author of Scripture and He knows the end from the beginning (Is 46:10).

UNDERSTAND IT WITHIN REDEMPTIVE HISTORY.

God revealed His plan of redemption a little bit at a time, rather than all at once. Therefore, important themes and theological concepts develop gradually from Genesis to Revelation. In addition, Old Testament writers often wrote about Christ but did not fully realize it (Jn 5:46; 1Pt 1:10–11). For this reason, some passages are beautifully layered with a basic meaning rooted in the original setting and a fuller meaning that can only be understood in light of Christ's work (1Co 10:1–4).

UNDERSTAND IT IN ITS MANY GENRES.

The Bible is a true story, but it's not all historical narrative. There are many types of literature in Scripture, including poetry, prophecy, legal codes, and letters. Just as we would not read song lyrics the same way we read a news article, we should allow each genre to speak to us in its own voice (Dt 32:2).

LIVE GOD'S WORD

Reading the Bible should not only be an opportunity to hear from God, but also an occasion to respond to Him in repentance and intercession, petition and praise. Many Christians have found praying the words of Scripture to be a powerful experience, especially in times of grief (Ps 56:4).

MAKE THE BIBLE A NECESSARY PART OF YOUR LIFE.

By making Scripture an ongoing part of everyday life, the Bible will transform our hearts and minds. Meditating on the Word of God regularly is key. In addition, memorizing individual verses and longer passages helps us internalize what we have read. The psalmist writes, "I have treasured your word in my heart, so that I may not sin against you" (Ps 119:11). When we memorize Scripture, we are better prepared for the trials of the Christian life (Mt 4:1–11).

BE A DOER OF THE WORD.

Jesus told His disciples, "Just as a branch is unable to produce fruit by itself unless it remains on the vine, neither can you unless you remain in me" (Jn 15:4). Our ongoing connection to Christ is essential if we are to live as He lived. Through His Word, God shapes us in order that we might do the good works He has prepared in advance for us to do (Jn 15:2, 7; Eph 2:10). We must be "doers of the word and not hearers only" (Jms 1:22), but it is Christ's power at work within us that allows us to "produce fruit."

THE BIBLE IS GOD'S STORY.

The Bible is about God's steadfast love for His people. It is about His sovereign plan, His grace, and His glory. You are meant to read it, and you are meant to be transformed by it.

PSALM 119: WE DELIGHT IN YOUR WORD

THE MIND SERVES BEST WHEN IT'S ANCHORED IN THE WORD OF GOD.

FLANNERY O'CONNOR

HAPPY ARE THOSE WHO KEEP HIS DECREES

Psalm 119:1–16
DELIGHT IN GOD'S WORD

ALEPH

¹ How happy are those whose way is blameless,
who walk according to the Lᴏʀᴅ's instruction!
² Happy are those who keep his decrees
and seek him with all their heart.
³ They do nothing wrong;
they walk in his ways.
⁴ You have commanded that your precepts
be diligently kept.
⁵ If only my ways were committed
to keeping your statutes!
⁶ Then I would not be ashamed
when I think about all your commands.
⁷ I will praise you with an upright heart
when I learn your righteous judgments.
⁸ I will keep your statutes;
never abandon me.

BETH

9 How can a young man keep his way pure?
By keeping your word.
10 I have sought you with all my heart;
don't let me wander from your commands.
11 I have treasured your word in my heart
so that I may not sin against you.
12 Lord, may you be blessed;
teach me your statutes.
13 With my lips I proclaim
all the judgments from your mouth.
14 I rejoice in the way revealed by your decrees
as much as in all riches.
15 I will meditate on your precepts
and think about your ways.
16 I will delight in your statutes;
I will not forget your word.

Psalm 19:7–8

7 The instruction of the Lord is perfect,
renewing one's life;
the testimony of the Lord is trustworthy,
making the inexperienced wise.
8 The precepts of the Lord are right,
making the heart glad;
the command of the Lord is radiant,
making the eyes light up.

results:
renewal of life
inexperienced wise
heart glad
eyes light up!!

Lord:
instruction- perfect
testimony - trustworthy
precepts - right
command - radiant

DELIGHT IN

DAY 1

THE WORD

Psalm 119 invites us to delight in the beauty, goodness, and truth found in God's Word. Take some time today to pause, reflect, and delight in Exodus 20:1–17.

EXODUS 20:1-17

THE TEN COMMANDMENTS

¹ Then God spoke all these words:

² I am the LORD your God, who brought you out of the land of Egypt, out of the place of slavery.

³ Do not have other gods besides me.

⁴ Do not make an idol for yourself, whether in the shape of anything in the heavens above or on the earth below or in the waters under the earth. ⁵ Do not bow in worship to them, and do not serve them; for I, the LORD your God, am a jealous God, punishing the children for the fathers' iniquity, to the third and fourth generations of those who hate me, ⁶ but showing faithful love to a thousand generations of those who love me and keep my commands.

⁷ Do not misuse the name of the LORD your God, because the LORD will not leave anyone unpunished who misuses his name.

⁸ Remember the Sabbath day, to keep it holy: ⁹ You are to labor six days and do all your work, ¹⁰ but the seventh day is a Sabbath to the LORD your God. You must not do any work—you, your son or daughter, your male or female servant, your livestock, or the resident alien who is within your city gates. ¹¹ For the LORD made the heavens and the earth, the sea, and everything in them in six days; then he rested on the seventh day. Therefore the LORD blessed the Sabbath day and declared it holy.

¹² Honor your father and your mother so that you may have a long life in the land that the LORD your God is giving you.

¹³ Do not murder.

¹⁴ Do not commit adultery.

¹⁵ Do not steal.

¹⁶ Do not give false testimony against your neighbor.

God spoke these words   wow!!

Do not have other God's besides me!

Holy sabbath.

¹⁷ Do not covet your neighbor's house. Do not covet your neighbor's wife, his male or female servant, his ox or donkey, or anything that belongs to your neighbor.

Do not   Make   no one will be
                       left unpunished.
            bow

            misuse

What would my other God's be?

        money   security

        comfort

DAY 2

GIVE ME LIFE THROUGH YOUR WORD

Psalm 119:17–32

GIMEL

¹⁷ Deal generously with your servant
so that I might live;
then I will keep your word.
¹⁸ Open my eyes so that I may contemplate
wondrous things from your instruction.
¹⁹ I am a resident alien on earth;
do not hide your commands from me.
²⁰ I am continually overcome
with longing for your judgments.
²¹ You rebuke the arrogant,
the ones under a curse,
who wander from your commands.
²² Take insult and contempt away from me,
for I have kept your decrees.
²³ Though princes sit together speaking against me,
your servant will think about your statutes;
²⁴ your decrees are my delight
and my counselors.

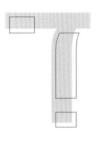

DALETH

²⁵ My life is down in the dust;
give me life through your word.
²⁶ I told you about my life,
and you answered me;
teach me your statutes.
²⁷ Help me understand
the meaning of your precepts
so that I can meditate on your wonders.
²⁸ I am weary from grief;
strengthen me through your word.
²⁹ Keep me from the way of deceit
and graciously give me your instruction.
³⁰ I have chosen the way of truth;
I have set your ordinances before me.
³¹ I cling to your decrees;
Lᴏʀᴅ, do not put me to shame.
³² I pursue the way of your commands,
for you broaden my understanding.

Joshua 1:6–8

⁶ "Be strong and courageous, for you will distribute the land I swore to their fathers to give them as an inheritance. ⁷ Above all, be strong and very courageous to observe carefully the whole instruction my servant Moses commanded you. Do not turn from it to the right or the left, so that you will have success wherever you go.

⁸ THIS BOOK OF INSTRUCTION MUST NOT DEPART FROM YOUR MOUTH; YOU ARE TO MEDITATE ON IT DAY AND NIGHT SO THAT YOU MAY CAREFULLY OBSERVE EVERYTHING WRITTEN IN IT.

For then you will prosper and succeed in whatever you do."

DELIGHT IN

THE WORD

Psalm 119 invites us to delight in the beauty, goodness, and truth found in God's Word. Take some time today to pause, reflect, and delight in Galatians 4:1–7.

GALATIANS 4:1–7

¹ Now I say that as long as the heir is a child, he differs in no way from a slave, though he is the owner of everything. ² Instead, he is under guardians and trustees until the time set by his father. ³ In the same way we also, when we were children, were in slavery under the elements of the world. ⁴ When the time came to completion, God sent his Son, born of a woman, born under the law, ⁵ to redeem those under the law, so that we might receive adoption as sons. ⁶ And because you are sons, God sent the Spirit of his Son into our hearts, crying, "*Abba*, Father!" ⁷ So you are no longer a slave but a son, and if a son, then God has made you an heir.

PAUSE, REFLECT & DELIGHT

THE WORD OF GOD

In the Bible, the phrases "the word of God,"
"the word of the LORD," or sometimes simply
"the word," are used to describe many of the
different ways God has revealed Himself.

THE

HIS SPOKEN WORD

EX 3:4–6

EX 20

HIS COMMANDS

WORD

SCRIPTURE

DT 27:3

HEB 4:1–13

HIS JUDGMENT

HIS WORDS SPOKEN BY PROPHETS

JR 43:1; HEB 1:1

OF

JN 1:1–5; HEB 1:2

THE SON OF GOD

JESUS'S TEACHINGS

MK 2:2

GOD

AC 13:49

THE GOSPEL MESSAGE

DAY 3

TEACH ME THE MEANING OF YOUR STATUTES

Psalm 119:33–56

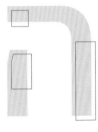

HE

³³ Teach me, LORD, the meaning of your statutes,
and I will always keep them.
³⁴ Help me understand your instruction,
and I will obey it
and follow it with all my heart. ♡
³⁵ Help me stay on the path of your commands,
for I take pleasure in it.
³⁶ Turn my heart to your decrees
and not to dishonest profit.
³⁷ Turn my eyes
from looking at what is worthless;
✳ give me life in your ways.
³⁸ Confirm what you said to your servant,
for it produces reverence for you.
³⁹ Turn away the disgrace I dread;
indeed, your judgments are good.
⁴⁰ How I long for your precepts!
✳ Give me life through your righteousness.

I do take pleasure on the path of your commands

WAW

⁴¹ Let your faithful love come to me, LORD,
your salvation, as you promised.
⁴² Then I can answer the one who taunts me,
for I trust in your word.
⁴³ Never take the word of truth from my mouth,
for I hope in your judgments.
⁴⁴ I will always obey your instruction,
forever and ever.
⁴⁵ I will walk freely in an open place
because I study your precepts.
⁴⁶ I will speak of your decrees before kings
and not be ashamed.
⁴⁷ I delight in your commands,
which I love.
⁴⁸ I will lift up my hands to your commands,
which I love,
and will meditate on your statutes.

ZAYIN

Help me to obey.....

⁴⁹ Remember your word to your servant;
you have given me hope through it.
⁵⁰ This is my comfort in my affliction:
Your promise has given me life.
⁵¹ The arrogant constantly ridicule me,
but I do not turn away from your instruction.
⁵² LORD, I remember your judgments from long ago
and find comfort.
⁵³ Rage seizes me because of the wicked
who reject your instruction.
⁵⁴ Your statutes are the theme of my song
during my earthly life.
⁵⁵ LORD, I remember your name in the night,
and I obey your instruction.
⁵⁶ This is my practice:
I obey your precepts.

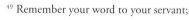

teach me
Help me
turn my heart
turn my eyes
confirm ....

give me life in your ways.
give me life through your
righteousness.

you have given me hope
through your word.

your promise has
given me life.

2 Timothy 3:16–17

¹⁶ All Scripture is inspired by God and is profitable for teaching, for rebuking, for correcting, for training in righteousness, ¹⁷ so that the man of God may be complete, equipped for every good work.

DELIGHT IN

THE WORD

Psalm 119 invites us to delight in the beauty, goodness, and truth found in God's Word. Take some time today to pause, reflect, and delight in James 1:16–25.

JAMES 1:16-25

16 Don't be deceived, my dear brothers and sisters. 17 Every good and perfect gift is from above, coming down from the Father of lights, who does not change like shifting shadows. 18 By his own choice, he gave us birth by the word of truth so that we would be a kind of firstfruits of his creatures.

HEARING AND DOING THE WORD

19 My dear brothers and sisters, understand this: Everyone should be quick to listen, slow to speak, and slow to anger, 20 for human anger does not accomplish God's righteousness. 21 Therefore, ridding yourselves of all moral filth and the evil that is so prevalent, humbly receive the implanted word, which is able to save your souls.

22 But be doers of the word and not hearers only, deceiving yourselves. 23 Because if anyone is a hearer of the word and not a doer, he is like someone looking at his own face in a mirror. 24 For he looks at himself, goes away, and immediately forgets what kind of person he was. 25 But the one who looks intently into the perfect law of freedom and perseveres in it, and is not a forgetful hearer but a doer who works—this person will be blessed in what he does.

PAUSE, REFLECT & DELIGHT

Every good & perfect gift is from above
God gave us birth by the Word of truth.
So that we would be a kind of firstfruits of his creatures

Quick to listen   humbly receive the
Slow to speak.   implanted word
Slow to anger

be doers of the word.
look intently into the perfect law of freedom
& preserve it.

BLESSED LORD, WHICH HAST CAUSED ALL HOLY SCRIPTURES
TO BE WRITTEN FOR OUR LEARNING; GRANT US THAT WE
MAY IN SUCH WISE HEAR THEM, READ, MARK, LEARN, AND
INWARDLY DIGEST THEM.

THOMAS CRANMER

I HAVE PROMISED TO KEEP YOUR WORDS

Psalm 119:57–72

CHETH

57 The LORD is my portion;
I have promised to keep your words.
58 I have sought your favor with all my heart;
be gracious to me according to your promise.
59 I thought about my ways
and turned my steps back to your decrees.
60 I hurried, not hesitating
to keep your commands.
61 Though the ropes of the wicked
were wrapped around me,
I did not forget your instruction.
62 I rise at midnight to thank you
for your righteous judgments.
63 I am a friend to all who fear you,
to those who keep your precepts.
64 LORD, the earth is filled with your faithful love;
teach me your statutes.

TETH

⁶⁵ Lᴏʀᴅ, you have treated your servant well,
just as you promised.
⁶⁶ Teach me good judgment and discernment,
for I rely on your commands.
⁶⁷ Before I was afflicted I went astray,
but now I keep your word.
⁶⁸ You are good, and you do what is good;
teach me your statutes.
⁶⁹ The arrogant have smeared me with lies,
but I obey your precepts with all my heart.
⁷⁰ Their hearts are hard and insensitive,
but I delight in your instruction.
⁷¹ It was good for me to be afflicted
so that I could learn your statutes.
⁷² Instruction from your lips is better for me
than thousands of gold and silver pieces.

Deuteronomy 6:6–9

⁶ These words that I am giving you today are to be in
your heart.

⁷ REPEAT THEM TO YOUR CHILDREN. TALK
ABOUT THEM WHEN YOU SIT IN YOUR
HOUSE AND WHEN YOU WALK ALONG THE
ROAD, WHEN YOU LIE DOWN AND WHEN
YOU GET UP.

⁸ Bind them as a sign on your hand and let them be a
symbol on your forehead. ⁹ Write them on the doorposts
of your house and on your city gates.

DELIGHT IN

THE WORD

Psalm 119 invites us to delight in the beauty, goodness, and truth found in God's Word. Take some time today to pause, reflect, and delight in Joshua 2:1–21.

JOSHUA 2:1–21

SPIES SENT TO JERICHO

¹ Joshua son of Nun secretly sent two men as spies from the Acacia Grove, saying, "Go and scout the land, especially Jericho." So they left, and they came to the house of a prostitute named Rahab, and stayed there.

² The king of Jericho was told, "Look, some of the Israelite men have come here tonight to investigate the land." ³ Then the king of Jericho sent word to Rahab and said, "Bring out the men who came to you and entered your house, for they came to investigate the entire land."

⁴ But the woman had taken the two men and hidden them. So she said, "Yes, the men did come to me, but I didn't know where they were from. ⁵ At nightfall, when the city gate was about to close, the men went out, and I don't know where they were going. Chase after them quickly, and you can catch up with them!" ⁶ But she had taken them up to the roof and hidden them among the stalks of flax that she had arranged on the roof. ⁷ The men pursued them along the road to the fords of the Jordan, and as soon as they left to pursue them, the city gate was shut.

THE PROMISE TO RAHAB

⁸ Before the men fell asleep, she went up on the roof ⁹ and said to them, "I know that the Lord has given you this land and that the terror of you has fallen on us, and everyone who lives in the land is panicking because of you. ¹⁰ For we have heard how the Lord dried up the water of the Red Sea before you when you came out of Egypt, and what you did to Sihon and Og, the two Amorite kings you completely destroyed across the Jordan. ¹¹ When we heard this, we lost heart, and everyone's courage failed because of you, for the Lord your God is God in heaven above and on earth below. ¹² Now please swear to me by the Lord that you will also show kindness to my father's family, because I showed kindness to you. Give me a sure sign ¹³ that you will spare the lives of my father, mother, brothers, sisters, and all who belong to them, and save us from death."

¹⁴ The men answered her, "We will give our lives for yours. If you don't report our mission, we will show kindness and faithfulness to you when the Lord gives us the land."

¹⁵ Then she let them down by a rope through the window, since she lived in a house that was built into the wall of the city. ¹⁶ "Go to the hill country so that the men pursuing you won't find you," she said to them. "Hide there for three days until they return; afterward, go on your way."

¹⁷ The men said to her, "We will be free from this oath you made us swear, ¹⁸ unless, when we enter the land, you tie this scarlet cord to the window through which you let us down. Bring your father, mother, brothers, and all your father's family into your house. ¹⁹ If anyone goes out the doors of your house, his death will be his own fault, and we will be innocent. But if anyone with you in the house should be harmed, his death will be our fault. ²⁰ And if you report our mission, we are free from the oath you made us swear."

²¹ "Let it be as you say," she replied, and she sent them away. After they had gone, she tied the scarlet cord to the window.

Keep your words
Keep your commands
Keep your precepts

teach me your statutes
teach me good judgment & discernment

I promise.
I obey.
I delight.
I rely,
I did not forget.

DAY 5

I PUT MY HOPE IN YOUR WORD

Psalm 119:73–88

YOD

73 Your hands made me and formed me;
give me understanding
so that I can learn your commands.
74 Those who fear you will see me and rejoice,
for I put my hope in your word.
75 I know, LORD, that your judgments are just
and that you have afflicted me fairly.
76 May your faithful love comfort me
as you promised your servant.
77 May your compassion come to me
so that I may live,
for your instruction is my delight.
78 Let the arrogant be put to shame
for slandering me with lies;
I will meditate on your precepts.
79 Let those who fear you,
those who know your decrees, turn to me.
80 May my heart be blameless regarding your statutes
so that I will not be put to shame.

KAPH

81 I long for your salvation;
I put my hope in your word.
82 My eyes grow weary
looking for what you have promised;
I ask, "When will you comfort me?"
83 Though I have become like a wineskin dried by smoke,
I do not forget your statutes.
84 How many days must your servant wait?
When will you execute judgment on my persecutors?
85 The arrogant have dug pits for me;
they violate your instruction.
86 All your commands are true;
people persecute me with lies—help me!
87 They almost ended my life on earth,
but I did not abandon your precepts.
88 Give me life in accordance with your faithful love,
and I will obey the decree you have spoken.

Hebrews 4:12–13

12 FOR THE WORD OF GOD IS LIVING AND
EFFECTIVE AND SHARPER THAN ANY DOUBLE-
EDGED SWORD,

penetrating as far as the separation of soul and spirit, joints
and marrow. It is able to judge the thoughts and intentions
of the heart. 13 No creature is hidden from him, but all things
are naked and exposed to the eyes of him to whom we must
give an account.

DELIGHT IN

DAY 5

THE WORD

Psalm 119 invites us to delight in the beauty, goodness, and truth found in God's Word. Take some time today to pause, reflect, and delight in Genesis 18:9–15 and 21:1–7.

GENESIS 18:9–15; 21:1–7

Genesis 18:9–15
SARAH LAUGHS

⁹ "Where is your wife Sarah?" they asked him.

"There, in the tent," he answered.

¹⁰ The Lord said, "I will certainly come back to you in about a year's time, and your wife Sarah will have a son!" Now Sarah was listening at the entrance of the tent behind him.

¹¹ Abraham and Sarah were old and getting on in years. Sarah had passed the age of childbearing. ¹² So she laughed to herself: "After I am worn out and my lord is old, will I have delight?"

¹³ But the Lord asked Abraham, "Why did Sarah laugh, saying, 'Can I really have a baby when I'm old?' ¹⁴ Is anything impossible for the Lord? At the appointed time I will come back to you, and in about a year she will have a son."

¹⁵ Sarah denied it. "I did not laugh," she said, because she was afraid.

But he replied, "No, you did laugh."

Genesis 21:1–7
THE BIRTH OF ISAAC

¹ The Lord came to Sarah as he had said, and the Lord did for Sarah what he had promised. ² Sarah became pregnant and bore a son to Abraham in his old age, at the appointed time God had told him. ³ Abraham named his son who was born to him—the one Sarah bore to him—Isaac. ⁴ When his son Isaac was eight days old, Abraham circumcised him, as God had commanded him. ⁵ Abraham was a hundred years old when his son Isaac was born to him.

⁶ Sarah said, "God has made me laugh, and everyone who hears will laugh with me." ⁷ She also said, "Who would have told Abraham that Sarah would nurse children? Yet I have borne a son for him in his old age."

PAUSE, REFLECT & DELIGHT

Take this day to catch up on your reading,
pray, and rest in the presence of the Lord.

THE INSTRUCTION OF THE LORD IS PERFECT, RENEWING ONE'S LIFE; THE TESTIMONY OF THE LORD IS TRUSTWORTHY, MAKING THE INEXPERIENCED WISE. THE PRECEPTS OF THE LORD ARE RIGHT, MAKING THE HEART GLAD; THE COMMAND OF THE LORD IS RADIANT, MAKING THE EYES LIGHT UP.

PSALM 19:7–8

WEEKLY TRUTH

Scripture is God-breathed and true. When we memorize it, we carry the good news of Jesus with us wherever we go.

As we read Psalm 119, we will memorize the key verse for this reading plan.

YOU ARE MY SHELTER AND MY SHIELD;
I PUT MY HOPE IN YOUR WORD.

PSALM 119:114

TO AID IN YOUR MEMORIZATION, COPY
PSALM 119:114 A FEW TIMES BELOW.

You are my shelter & my shield;
I put my hope in your word.

NOBODY EVER OUTGROWS SCRIPTURE; THE BOOK
WIDENS AND DEEPENS WITH OUR YEARS.

CHARLES SPURGEON

DAY 8

YOUR WORD IS FOREVER

Psalm 119:89–104

LAMED

89 LORD, your word is forever;
it is firmly fixed in heaven.
90 Your faithfulness is for all generations;
you established the earth, and it stands firm.
91 Your judgments stand firm today,
for all things are your servants.
92 If your instruction had not been my delight,
I would have died in my affliction.
93 I will never forget your precepts,
for you have given me life through them.
94 I am yours; save me,
for I have studied your precepts.
95 The wicked hope to destroy me,
but I contemplate your decrees.
96 I have seen a limit to all perfection,
but your command is without limit.

MEM

⁹⁷ How I love your instruction!
It is my meditation all day long.
⁹⁸ Your commands make me wiser than my enemies,
for they are always with me.
⁹⁹ I have more insight than all my teachers
because your decrees are my meditation.
¹⁰⁰ I understand more than the elders
because I obey your precepts.
¹⁰¹ I have kept my feet from every evil path
to follow your word.
¹⁰² I have not turned from your judgments,
for you yourself have instructed me.
¹⁰³ How sweet your word is to my taste—
sweeter than honey in my mouth.
¹⁰⁴ I gain understanding from your precepts;
therefore I hate every false way.

your word:
- *is forever*
- *Follow it*
- *sweet to taste*
- *remains forever.*

Isaiah 40:6–8

⁶ A voice was saying, "Cry out!"
Another said, "What should I cry out?"
"All humanity is grass,
and all its goodness is like the flower of the field.
⁷ The grass withers, the flowers fade
when the breath of the Lᴏʀᴅ blows on them;
indeed, the people are grass.

⁸ THE GRASS WITHERS, THE
   FLOWERS FADE,
BUT THE WORD OF OUR GOD
   REMAINS FOREVER."

meditate:
God's instructions
God's decrees

God's precepts:
- *never forget*
- *study them*
- *obey them*
- *gain understanding*

DELIGHT IN

DAY 8

THE WORD

Psalm 119 invites us to delight in the beauty, goodness, and truth found in God's Word. Take some time today to pause, reflect, and delight in Isaiah 41:17–20.

ISAIAH 41:17–20

[17] "The poor and the needy seek water, but there is none;
their tongues are parched with thirst.
I will answer them.
I am the LORD, the God of Israel. I will not abandon them.
[18] I will open rivers on the barren heights,
and springs in the middle of the plains.
I will turn the desert into a pool
and dry land into springs.
[19] I will plant cedars,
acacias, myrtles, and olive trees in the wilderness.
I will put juniper trees,
elms, and cypress trees together in the desert,
[20] so that all may see and know,
consider and understand,
that the hand of the LORD has done this,
the Holy One of Israel has created it."

PAUSE, REFLECT & DELIGHT

God will answer the poor & need.

YOUR WORD IS A LAMP FOR MY FEET

Psalm 119:105–120

NUN

¹⁰⁵ Your word is a lamp for my feet
and a light on my path.
¹⁰⁶ I have solemnly sworn
to keep your righteous judgments.
¹⁰⁷ I am severely afflicted;
Lᴏʀᴅ, give me life according to your word.
¹⁰⁸ Lᴏʀᴅ, please accept my freewill offerings of praise,
and teach me your judgments. ♡
¹⁰⁹ My life is constantly in danger,
yet I do not forget your instruction.
¹¹⁰ The wicked have set a trap for me,
but I have not wandered from your precepts.
¹¹¹ I have your decrees as a heritage forever;
indeed, they are the joy of my heart. ♡
¹¹² I am resolved to obey your statutes
to the very end.

SAMEK

¹¹³ I hate those who are double-minded,
but I love your instruction.
¹¹⁴ You are my shelter and my shield;
I put my hope in your word.
¹¹⁵ Depart from me, you evil ones,
so that I may obey my God's commands.
¹¹⁶ Sustain me as you promised, and I will live;
do not let me be ashamed of my hope.
¹¹⁷ Sustain me so that I can be safe
and always be concerned about your statutes.
¹¹⁸ You reject all who stray from your statutes,
for their deceit is a lie.
¹¹⁹ You remove all the wicked on earth
as if they were dross from metal;
therefore, I love your decrees.
¹²⁰ I tremble in awe of you;
I fear your judgments.

Proverbs 19:21

Many plans are in a person's heart,
but the LORD's decree will prevail.

AMEN!

DELIGHT IN

THE WORD

Psalm 119 invites us to delight in the beauty, goodness, and truth found in God's Word. Take some time today to pause, reflect, and delight in 1 Chronicles 28:9–20.

1 CHRONICLES 28:9-20

9 "As for you, Solomon my son, know the God of your father, and serve him wholeheartedly and with a willing mind, for the LORD searches every heart and understands the intention of every thought. If you seek him, he will be found by you, but if you abandon him, he will reject you forever. 10 Realize now that the LORD has chosen you to build a house for the sanctuary. Be strong, and do it."

11 Then David gave his son Solomon the plans for the portico of the temple and its buildings, treasuries, upstairs rooms, inner rooms, and a room for the mercy seat. 12 The plans contained everything he had in mind for the courts of the LORD's house, all the surrounding chambers, the treasuries of God's house, and the treasuries for what is dedicated. 13 Also included were plans for the divisions of the priests and the Levites; all the work of service in the LORD's house; all the articles of service of the LORD's house; 14 the weight of gold for all the articles for every kind of service; the weight of all the silver articles for every kind of service; 15 the weight of the gold lampstands and their gold lamps, including the weight of each lampstand and its lamps; the weight of each silver lampstand and its lamps, according to the service of each lampstand; 16 the weight of gold for each table for the rows of the Bread of the Presence and the silver for the silver tables; 17 the pure gold for the forks, sprinkling basins, and pitchers; the weight of each gold dish; the weight of each silver bowl; 18 the weight of refined gold for the altar of incense; and the plans for the chariot of the gold cherubim that spread out their wings and cover the ark of the LORD's covenant.

19 David concluded, "By the LORD's hand on me, he enabled me to understand everything in writing, all the details of the plan."

20 Then David said to his son Solomon, "Be strong and courageous, and do the work. Don't be afraid or discouraged, for the LORD God, my God, is with you. He won't leave you or abandon you until all the work for the service of the LORD's house is finished."

PAUSE, REFLECT & DELIGHT

the lord searches every heart &
understands the intention of every thought.

your decrees are the joy of my heart.

Many plans are in a person's heart
but the Lord's decree will prevail

DAY 10

YOUR DECREES ARE WONDROUS

Psalm 119:121–144

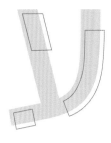

AYIN

¹²¹ I have done what is just and right;
do not leave me to my oppressors.
¹²² Guarantee your servant's well-being;
do not let the arrogant oppress me.
¹²³ My eyes grow weary looking for your salvation
and for your righteous promise.
¹²⁴ Deal with your servant based on your faithful love;
teach me your statutes.
¹²⁵ I am your servant; give me understanding
so that I may know your decrees.
¹²⁶ It is time for the LORD to act,
for they have violated your instruction.
¹²⁷ Since I love your commands
more than gold, even the purest gold,
¹²⁸ I carefully follow all your precepts
and hate every false way.

PE

¹²⁹ Your decrees are wondrous;
therefore I obey them.
¹³⁰ The revelation of your words brings light
and gives understanding to the inexperienced.
¹³¹ I open my mouth and pant
because I long for your commands.
¹³² Turn to me and be gracious to me,
as is your practice toward those who love your name.
¹³³ Make my steps steady through your promise;
don't let any sin dominate me.
¹³⁴ Redeem me from human oppression,
and I will keep your precepts.
¹³⁵ Make your face shine on your servant,
and teach me your statutes.
¹³⁶ My eyes pour out streams of tears
because people do not follow your instruction.

TSADE

¹³⁷ You are righteous, LORD,
and your judgments are just.
¹³⁸ The decrees you issue are righteous
and altogether trustworthy.
¹³⁹ My anger overwhelms me
because my foes forget your words.
¹⁴⁰ Your word is completely pure,
and your servant loves it.
¹⁴¹ I am insignificant and despised,
but I do not forget your precepts.
¹⁴² Your righteousness is an everlasting righteousness,
and your instruction is true.
¹⁴³ Trouble and distress have overtaken me,
but your commands are my delight.
¹⁴⁴ Your decrees are righteous forever.
Give me understanding, and I will live.

Romans 15:4

For whatever was written in the past was written for our instruction, so that we may have hope through endurance and through the encouragement from the Scriptures.

DELIGHT IN

THE WORD

Psalm 119 invites us to delight in the beauty, goodness, and truth found in God's Word. Take some time today to pause, reflect, and delight in 1 Corinthians 13.

1 CORINTHIANS 13

[1] If I speak human or angelic tongues but do not have love, I am a noisy gong or a clanging cymbal. [2] If I have the gift of prophecy and understand all mysteries and all knowledge, and if I have all faith so that I can move mountains but do not have love, I am nothing. [3] And if I give away all my possessions, and if I give over my body in order to boast but do not have love, I gain nothing.

[4] Love is patient, love is kind. Love does not envy, is not boastful, is not arrogant, [5] is not rude, is not self-seeking, is not irritable, and does not keep a record of wrongs. [6] Love finds no joy in unrighteousness but rejoices in the truth. [7] It bears all things, believes all things, hopes all things, endures all things.

[8] Love never ends. But as for prophecies, they will come to an end; as for tongues, they will cease; as for knowledge, it will come to an end. [9] For we know in part, and we prophesy in part, [10] but when the perfect comes, the partial will come to an end. [11] When I was a child, I spoke like a child, I thought like a child, I reasoned like a child. When I became a man, I put aside childish things. [12] For now we see only a reflection as in a mirror, but then face to face. Now I know in part, but then I will know fully, as I am fully known. [13] Now these three remain: faith, hope, and love—but the greatest of these is love.

PAUSE, REFLECT & DELIGHT

give me understanding. 2X
teach me your statutes 2X

Lots of things I say I do	Lots of requests of God
I have done what is just & right	do not leave me
I am your servant.	guarantee your servant's well being
I may know your decrees	give me understanding 2X
I love your commands	turn to me
I carefully follow All your precepts	be gracious to me.
I obey them	make my steps steady
I long for your commands	don't let sin dominate me.
I will keep your precepts	make your face shine on your servant.
I do not forget your precepts	
I will live.	

THE HISTORY
OF THE BIBLE

The Bible is one complete work, made up of sixty-six smaller works written over more than fifteen centuries in a variety of genres. Each smaller book was originally read from a scroll, written on papyrus (a paper-like material made from the papyrus reed) or vellum (made from cow or goat skins). Each separate text was eventually transcribed onto sheets of paper and bound into a single codex, a book with pages similar to what we read today.

THE FOLLOWING PAGES CONTAIN A TIMELINE OF SOME
IMPORTANT DATES IN THE HISTORY OF THE BIBLE.

THIRD AND SECOND CENTURIES BC

The Old Testament is translated into Greek. This translation is called the Septuagint and is read in synagogues from the intertestamental period into the second century AD.

The Septuagint is the Old Testament used by the early Christians living in the Greco-Roman world.

AD 367

Athanasius writes an Easter letter with the first complete list of the official books included in the New Testament canon.

1440 TO 300 BC

The thirty-nine books of the Old Testament are written in Hebrew, with some portions in Aramaic.

AD 405

Jerome translates the Hebrew and Greek scriptures into Latin, creating the Vulgate.

AD 48 TO 95

The twenty-seven books of the New Testament are written in Greek, with some transliterated Aramaic words and phrases.

BC

AD

1350–350 BC

1500 BC

0

AD 500

AD 1382

John Wycliffe finishes the first translation of the Bible into English.

Since it was translated before the invention of the printing press, it would have been written by hand.

AD 1455

The first Bible is printed on Gutenberg's printing press.

In 1987, a copy of this Bible sold for more than two million dollars.

AD 1947

A young shepherd boy discovers the Dead Sea Scrolls (over nine hundred preserved manuscripts in Hebrew, Aramaic, and Greek) hidden in the caves of Qumran, twenty miles outside of Jerusalem. Included in this discovery were copies of almost every book from the Old Testament.

These ancient scrolls are more than a thousand years older than what had previously been considered the oldest existing manuscripts.

AD 1534

Martin Luther finishes his translation of the Bible into German from the original Greek and Hebrew.

AD 1150 TO 1228

Archbishop of Canterbury Stephen Langton divides the books of the Bible into chapters for the first time.

AD 1551

Robert Estienne, a printer in Switzerland, prints the first copy of the New Testament with verse numbers.

AD 2008

The first mobile Bible app launches for the Apple iPhone.

AD 1611

The King James Version of the Bible is produced in England.

AD 1663

The first Bible printed in America is an Algonquin translation of the text by pastor John Eliot.

AD 2019

The complete Bible is translated into its 698th language.

AD 1000

AD 1500

AD 2000

I HAVE NOT FORGOTTEN YOUR INSTRUCTION

Psalm 119:145–160

QOPH

[145] I call with all my heart; answer me, LORD.
I will obey your statutes.
[146] I call to you; save me,
and I will keep your decrees.
[147] I rise before dawn and cry out for help;
I put my hope in your word.
[148] I am awake through each watch of the night
to meditate on your promise.
[149] In keeping with your faithful love, hear my voice.
LORD, give me life in keeping with your justice.
[150] Those who pursue evil plans come near;
they are far from your instruction.
[151] You are near, LORD,
and all your commands are true.
[152] Long ago I learned from your decrees
that you have established them forever.

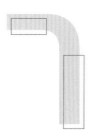

RESH

¹⁵³ Consider my affliction and rescue me,
for I have not forgotten your instruction.
¹⁵⁴ Champion my cause and redeem me;
give me life as you promised.
¹⁵⁵ Salvation is far from the wicked
because they do not study your statutes.
¹⁵⁶ Your compassions are many, LORD;
give me life according to your judgments.
¹⁵⁷ My persecutors and foes are many.
I have not turned from your decrees.
¹⁵⁸ I have seen the disloyal and feel disgust
because they do not keep your word.
¹⁵⁹ Consider how I love your precepts;
LORD, give me life according to your faithful love.
¹⁶⁰ The entirety of your word is truth,
each of your righteous judgments endures forever.

Romans 2:12–13

¹² All who sin without the law will also perish without the law, and all who sin under the law will be judged by the law. ¹³ For the hearers of the law are not righteous before God, but the doers of the law will be justified.

DELIGHT IN

THE WORD

Psalm 119 invites us to delight in the beauty, goodness, and truth found in God's Word. Take some time today to pause, reflect, and delight in Ecclesiastes 2:24–25.

ECCLESIASTES 2:24–25

[24] There is nothing better for a person than to eat, drink, and enjoy his work. I have seen that even this is from God's hand, [25] because who can eat and who can enjoy life apart from him?

PAUSE, REFLECT & DELIGHT

MY HEART FEARS ONLY YOUR WORD

Psalm 119:161–176

SIN/SHIN

161 Princes have persecuted me without cause,
but my heart fears only your word.
162 I rejoice over your promise
like one who finds vast treasure.
163 I hate and abhor falsehood,
but I love your instruction.
164 I praise you seven times a day
for your righteous judgments.
165 Abundant peace belongs to those
who love your instruction;
nothing makes them stumble.
166 Lord, I hope for your salvation
and carry out your commands.
167 I obey your decrees
and love them greatly.
168 I obey your precepts and decrees,
for all my ways are before you.

TAW

¹⁶⁹ Let my cry reach you, LORD;

give me understanding according to your word.

¹⁷⁰ Let my plea reach you;

rescue me according to your promise.

¹⁷¹ My lips pour out praise,

for you teach me your statutes.

¹⁷² My tongue sings about your promise,

for all your commands are righteous.

¹⁷³ May your hand be ready to help me,

for I have chosen your precepts.

¹⁷⁴ I long for your salvation, LORD,

and your instruction is my delight.

¹⁷⁵ Let me live, and I will praise you;

may your judgments help me.

¹⁷⁶ I wander like a lost sheep;

seek your servant,

for I do not forget your commands.

Ecclesiastes 12:12–14

¹² But beyond these, my son, be warned: there is no end to the making of many books, and much study wearies the body. ¹³ When all has been heard, the conclusion of the matter is this: fear God and keep his commands, because this is for all humanity. ¹⁴ For God will bring every act to judgment, including every hidden thing, whether good or evil.

DELIGHT IN

THE WORD

Psalm 119 invites us to delight in the beauty, goodness, and truth found in God's Word. Take some time today to pause, reflect, and delight in John 21:1–19.

JOHN 21:1–19

JESUS'S THIRD APPEARANCE TO THE DISCIPLES

[1] After this, Jesus revealed himself again to his disciples by the Sea of Tiberias. He revealed himself in this way:

[2] Simon Peter, Thomas (called "Twin"), Nathanael from Cana of Galilee, Zebedee's sons, and two others of his disciples were together.

[3] "I'm going fishing," Simon Peter said to them.

"We're coming with you," they told him. They went out and got into the boat, but that night they caught nothing.

[4] When daybreak came, Jesus stood on the shore, but the disciples did not know it was Jesus. [5] "Friends," Jesus called to them, "you don't have any fish, do you?"

"No," they answered.

[6] "Cast the net on the right side of the boat," he told them, "and you'll find some." So they did, and they were unable to haul it in because of the large number of fish. [7] The disciple, the one Jesus loved, said to Peter, "It is the Lord!"

When Simon Peter heard that it was the Lord, he tied his outer clothing around him (for he had taken it off) and plunged into the sea. [8] Since they were not far from land (about a hundred yards away), the other disciples came in the boat, dragging the net full of fish.

[9] When they got out on land, they saw a charcoal fire there, with fish lying on it, and bread. [10] "Bring some of the fish you've just caught," Jesus told them. [11] So Simon Peter climbed up and hauled the net ashore, full of large fish—153 of them. Even though there were so many, the net was not torn.

[12] "Come and have breakfast," Jesus told them. None of the disciples dared ask him, "Who are you?" because they knew it was the Lord. [13] Jesus came, took the bread, and gave it to them. He did the same with the fish. [14] This was now the third time Jesus appeared to the disciples after he was raised from the dead.

JESUS'S THREEFOLD RESTORATION OF PETER

[15] When they had eaten breakfast, Jesus asked Simon Peter, "Simon, son of John, do you love me more than these?"

"Yes, Lord," he said to him, "you know that I love you."

"Feed my lambs," he told him. [16] A second time he asked him, "Simon, son of John, do you love me?"

"Yes, Lord," he said to him, "you know that I love you."

"Shepherd my sheep," he told him.

[17] He asked him the third time, "Simon, son of John, do you love me?"

Peter was grieved that he asked him the third time, "Do you love me?" He said, "Lord, you know everything; you know that I love you."

"Feed my sheep," Jesus said. [18] "Truly I tell you, when you were younger, you would tie your belt and walk wherever you wanted. But when you grow old, you will stretch out your hands and someone else will tie you and carry you where you don't want to go." [19] He said this to indicate by what kind of death Peter would glorify God. After saying this, he told him, "Follow me."

Take this day to catch up on your reading,
pray, and rest in the presence of the Lord.

THE GRASS WITHERS, THE FLOWERS FADE,
BUT THE WORD OF OUR GOD REMAINS FOREVER.

ISAIAH 40:8

WEEKLY TRUTH

Scripture is God-breathed and true. When we memorize it, we carry the good news of Jesus with us wherever we go.

As we read Psalm 119, we will memorize the key verse for this reading plan.

YOU ARE MY SHELTER AND MY SHIELD;
I PUT MY HOPE IN YOUR WORD.

PSALM 119:114

TO AID IN YOUR MEMORIZATION, COPY
PSALM 119:114 A FEW TIMES BELOW.

OH, GIVE ME THAT BOOK! AT ANY PRICE, GIVE ME THE BOOK OF GOD!

"A MAN OF

I HAVE IT: HERE IS KNOWLEDGE ENOUGH FOR ME. LET ME BE:

ONE BOOK."

JOHN WESLEY

DOWNLOAD THE APP

VISIT
shereadstruth.com

SHOP
shopshereadstruth.com

CONTACT
hello@shereadstruth.com

CONNECT
@shereadstruth
#shereadstruth

LISTEN
She Reads Truth Podcast

CSB BOOK ABBREVIATIONS

OLD TESTAMENT

Genesis – Gn
Exodus – Ex
Leviticus – Lv
Numbers – Nm
Deuteronomy – Dt
Joshua – Jos
Judges – Jdg
Ruth – Ru
1 Samuel – 1Sm
2 Samuel – 2Sm
1 Kings – 1Kg
2 Kings – 2Kg
1 Chronicles – 1Ch
2 Chronicles – 2Ch
Ezra – Ezr
Nehemiah – Neh
Esther – Est
Job – Jb
Psalms – Ps
Proverbs – Pr
Ecclesiastes – Ec
Song of Solomon – Sg

Isaiah – Is
Jeremiah – Jr
Lamentations – Lm
Ezekiel – Ezk
Daniel – Dn
Hosea – Hs
Joel – Jl
Amos – Am
Obadiah – Ob
Jonah – Jnh
Micah – Mc
Nahum – Nah
Habakkuk – Hab
Zephaniah – Zph
Haggai – Hg
Zechariah – Zch
Malachi – Mal

NEW TESTAMENT

Matthew – Mt
Mark – Mk
Luke – Lk
John – Jn

Acts – Ac
Romans – Rm
1 Corinthians – 1Co
2 Corinthians – 2Co
Galatians – Gl
Ephesians – Eph
Philippians – Php
Colossians – Col
1 Thessalonians – 1Th
2 Thessalonians – 2Th
1 Timothy – 1Tm
2 Timothy – 2Tm
Titus – Ti
Philemon – Phm
Hebrews – Heb
James – Jms
1 Peter – 1Pt
2 Peter – 2Pt
1 John – 1Jn
2 John – 2Jn
3 John – 3Jn
Jude – Jd
Revelation – Rv

SHE
READS
TRUTH
PODCAST

Everything we do at She Reads Truth, including our podcast, supports one simple but powerful mission: women in the Word of God every day.

Join us in a weekly conversation with our founders, Raechel and Amanda, as they explore the beauty, goodness, and truth of Scripture. The She Reads Truth podcast was created as a companion resource to the She Reads Truth reading plans, Study Books, and devotionals. We hope this resource enhances your time in the Word.

JOIN US ON APPLE PODCASTS OR YOUR PREFERRED STREAMING PLATFORM

CONTINUE STUDYING THE PSALMS

God's people have used the Psalms as a guide for worship and prayer since before the time of Christ. The range of emotions found in the Psalms helps us find ways to express ourselves to God in every circumstance. In times of grief, joy, anxiety, and sorrow, the Psalms give us words for our emotions when we cannot find them on our own.

In our classic **Psalms for Prayer** Study Book, you will read and pray through a selection of fifteen psalms to use for prayer. Each day includes an interactive worksheet to guide you through prayer topics from praising God for His greatness to seeking His restful comfort.

FOR THE RECORD

WHERE DID I STUDY?

- O HOME
- O OFFICE
- O COFFEE SHOP
- O CHURCH
- O A FRIEND'S HOUSE
- O OTHER:

WHAT WAS I LISTENING TO?

ARTIST:

SONG:

PLAYLIST:

WHEN DID I STUDY?

MORNING

AFTERNOON

NIGHT

How did I find delight in God's Word?

WHAT WAS HAPPENING IN MY LIFE?

WHAT WAS HAPPENING IN THE WORLD?

MONTH	DAY	YEAR

END DATE